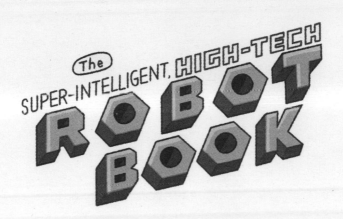

The SUPER-INTELLIGENT, HIGH-TECH ROBOT BOOK

Jon Milton is a science communicator who takes complex scientific theories and breaks them down into accessible bite-sized chunks. He works as part of science-comedy act Punk Science for the Science Museum in London and uses those skills to develop and perform shows on science, technology and engineering all over the world. He presented the TV series *Scien-trific* for Discovery and has performed his unique combination of science and comedy at venues across the globe from Ferrari World to Buckingham Palace.

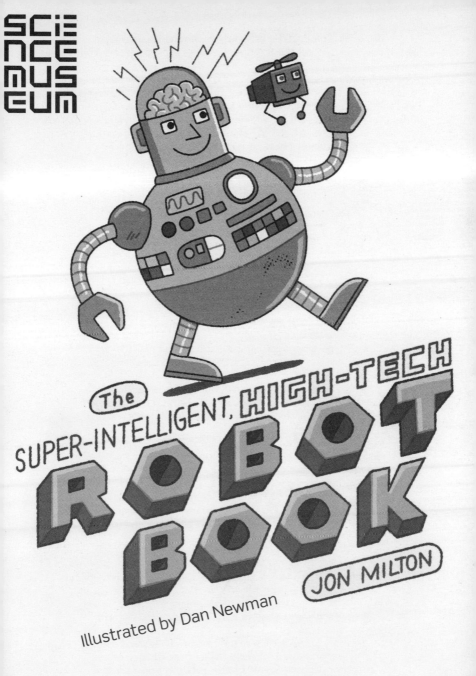

The SUPER-INTELLIGENT, HIGH-TECH ROBOT BOOK

JON MILTON

Illustrated by Dan Newman

MACMILLAN CHILDREN'S BOOKS

This book is produced in association with the Science Museum.
Sales of this book support the Science Museum's exhibitions and programmes.

Internationally recognized as one of the world's leading science centres,
the Science Museum, London, contains more than 10,000 amazing exhibits,
two fantastic simulator rides and the astounding IMAX cinema. Enter a world
of discovery and achievement, where you can see, touch and experience real
objects and icons which have shaped the world we live in today or
visit www.sciencemuseum.org.uk to find out more.

First published 2017 by Macmillan Children's Books
an imprint of Pan Macmillan
20 New Wharf Road, London N1 9RR
Associated companies throughout the world
www.panmacmillan.com

ISBN 978-1-5098-4235-3

1 3 5 7 9 8 6 4 2

A CIP catalogue record for this book is available from the British Library.

Designed by Dan Newman
Printed and bound by CPI Group (UK) Ltd, Croydon CR0 4YY

Contents

This one is for Mrs Milton

With thanks to Gaby Morgan, Wendy Burford, Ben Russell, Beth Linfield, Kenny Webster, Sam Furniss and Nicola

What is a Robot?

'm not going to tell you straight away. The idea is
that you have a think about what you imagine a robot
actually is.

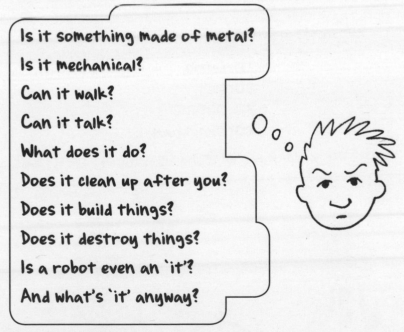

Is it something made of metal?

Is it mechanical?

Can it walk?

Can it talk?

What does it do?

Does it clean up after you?

Does it build things?

Does it destroy things?

Is a robot even an `it'?

And what's `it' anyway?

Too many questions? Sorry, that was another one.
Let's take a breath, do some light stretches and turn
the page.

Here's the first thing you need to know.

Robots are **awesome**. OK, that's not really an answer.

Robots are lots of different things. They are mechanical. They tend to do things for humans and sometimes they do them faster, more accurately, or for longer than a human can. Sometimes they do jobs that are just too dangerous for humans to do. All of these things put together are sometimes referred to as the 4 D's . . .

1D: Dumb
2D: Dull
3D: Dirty
4D: Dangerous

If a task is any of these 4 D's then it's probably better to get a robot to do it.

These 4D tasks range from repeating the same action thousands of times, over and over again, in a factory, to diving to the bottom of the deepest ocean to explore the seabed.

We're pretty used to seeing machines around us that have been programmed to carry out tasks, like washing machines, dishwashers or even cars that can park themselves. But are these robots? Not really, but they are pretty close to being robots because they are programmed to do jobs that would be boring or repetitive for us humans to do.

You might even have a robot of your own at home that you have built or that you program to do things. Robots are increasingly becoming part of our daily lives and aren't just for us to play with. They can build cars, clean the house, mow the lawn, help surgeons operate on us and even go into space. Oh, and did I mention they can walk, talk, fly, swim and even play musical instruments?

Robots are incredible things but they still need humans to help them.

They need to be told what to do by humans, at least to start with (some robots can learn things themselves).

Robots can look like humans or they can simply be a box on wheels, it depends on what their jobs are.

Robots got their name not from a scientist, but from a playwright. The word 'robota' first appeared in Karel Čapek's play *Rossum's Universal Robots* in 1920 and it was the Czech word for 'serf' or 'drudgery' which doesn't sound particularly good. If anything, it sounds a bit miserable. The play is about artificial humans, 'robota', who are forced to work for humans until they rise up and destroy the human race.

It's not exactly a happy tale but that's where the name **robot** comes from.

But it didn't actually have robots in it; it had actors dressed up as robots. Although robots dressed up as actors would have been better.

So, this may lead you into thinking that robots are about

a hundred years old. Which, considering the facts that you have been given above, would seem a pretty sensible conclusion and you're a pretty clever type of person . . . However, robots have been around for hundreds of years. They might not have been super-sophisticated like they are now but they were robots nonetheless.

Robots existed in Ancient Greece!

Yes, that is big news, and no, it's not a lie. This is a lie:

Underpants can be used as parachutes.

And that's not entirely a lie, if the underpants were big enough you could . . . Ahem, back to robots.

Robots have been around for over 2,000 years. To find out more turn the page now . . .

Please wait . . . robot-book loading next page. Next page loaded.

The Rise of the Robots

The very early robots are quite a bit different from the robots of today. The main difference being they weren't electronic; they were mechanical. Electronic robots need wires and circuits as well as electricity to power them. A mechanical robot relies on machinery and needs its energy to be stored in springs. No batteries, no plugging them into a socket. They were driven by cogs, gears, pulleys, cams, wheels and falling weights. They weren't originally called robots. That name didn't catch on until much later on. In the old days the ancestors of today's robots were called 'automatons', which means 'acting of one's own will', because they did stuff on their own.

But what were automatons for?

To make people go WOW! Plain and simple. They didn't do anything apart from entertain people.

They were a bit like the latest smartphone or a new pair of trainers: you don't really need them but they are all about showing off.

One automaton was called **The Writer**. It was built by Pierre and Henri Jaquet-Droz in the 1770s and it could actually write things.

Wait a second! How does an automaton write a letter? It's mechanical!

Simple. It just needs to have its movements programmed in a certain way.

You might be familiar with programming like **Scratch**. Scratch is a programming language that's easy to use because you use blocks with the instructions on them rather than writing loads of words and symbols. One block might be the instruction to take one step forward, one to turn right, etc., by building a chain of blocks you can program a sequence of movements. But what if Scratch was old school, what if it was mechanical not digital?

Cogs, **gears**, **pulleys**, **cams** and **wheels** were placed in particular sequences to make the parts of The Writer move in particular ways.

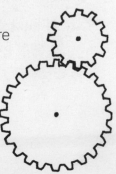

The Writer looks like a boy writing a note but inside it are 6,000 parts.

To understand how The Writer and indeed pretty much every other automaton worked we need to understand the parts that went into making it. People probably loved automatons like The Writer so much because even though they were amazing works of engineering they must have appeared to have been magical.

But they didn't run on magic, they used cogs, cams, gears, pulleys and wheels?

Hopefully you know what a wheel is, but if not they're in the shape of a circle and they make it easier to move

+++ 🗉 +++

things. For example, if you take the wheel off a wheelbarrow you just have a barrow and a lot of hard pushing to do.

But what about that other stuff – gulleys, pogs, cams and pears?

I think you mean pulleys, cogs, cams and gears. They have been around for centuries helping us humans do things more easily, whether it was your great-great-great-great-great-great-great-grandmother using a pulley to help her get water from a well or your great-great-great-great-great-great-uncle twice-removed grinding grain in a windmill.

This was state-of-the-art technology in its time. Just as the modern technology we see in a smartphone is similar to that in a modern robot, in the past the technology used by people every day was the same technology that made early robots work.

We'll start with the humble **cogwheel**. Like all these mechanical parts, its job is to make things easier to do. Cogwheels are very closely linked to **gears** – actually they're literally linked to them. They were first recorded as being used in China in the fourth century BC.

What were they used for?

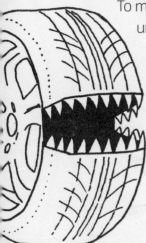

To make mills work more efficiently. And to understand how they do that, we need to learn a bit more about them.

A cogwheel is a wheel with **teeth** on it. Not human teeth, that would be weird. Metal teeth. They look like this. The teeth are called cogs.

They connect with another cogwheel or gear like this.

You'll have seen gears on a bike or experienced what they do in a car. Gears are very simple machines that make things easier to do.

If you connect a small gear to a bigger gear you'll get more force. This is what happens on a bike when you go up a steep hill.

If you want more speed, you need a big wheel driving a small wheel like this:

Turn the handle slowly and the beaters whizz round - because of gears.

The oldest working mechanical clock is in Salisbury Cathedral and dates back to 1326. It uses gears to work, which proves they must be rather reliable.

The Victorians loved gears. This machine made bricks.

The other important thing is a **pulley**. Pulleys need wheels to work and they look like this.

Pulleys reduce the amount of force you need to lift something. When the rope loops around the wheel, it changes the direction of the force and, because you are pulling down, you can also use your own body weight to help you.

But how does it work?

By redirecting and multiplying **force**. Force is either a push or a pull.

Imagine you have a 10kg block attached to a rope that you need to lift. The rope goes around the four wheels which reduces the amount of force you need to pull it up. It's called **mechanical advantage**.

It doesn't come for free, though, because you have to pull the rope a greater distance. Pulling up the rope by 1 metre means you have had to pull 4 metres of rope.

The use of pulleys dates back to 1500 BC in Mesopotamia, where they were used to hoist water from wells.

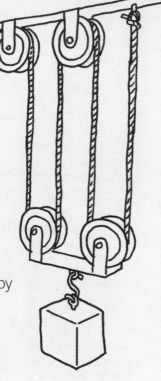

This arrangement takes a quarter of the effort, but you pull four times as long.

The famous Greek genius **Archimedes** is reported to have used pulleys to move a warship on his own.

But it's cams that do the special stuff?

Cams were reported to have been used in very old automatons that were made in Greece back in the third century BC.

A 'cam' is a piece of metal or other hard material, which looks like this:

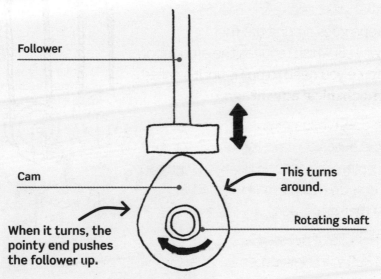

Follower

Cam

This turns around.

When it turns, the pointy end pushes the follower up.

Rotating shaft

Cams can come in lots of different shapes and sizes and are fixed to a shaft that rotates.

You also need a **follower**. No, not someone on Twitter. A follower is a rod. No, not someone called Rod. Just a rod.

The rod follows the edge of the cam. When the cam sticks out the rod moves up. When the cam has a dip the rod moves down.

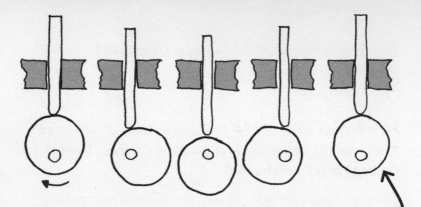

It's this movement that moves The Writer's arms. It's complicated though. You can't use just one cam; you have to use lots of cams in a programmed sequence to get the movement just right so what it writes looks like real handwriting.

The more cams you have the more instructions the automaton is given.

It's a seriously sophisticated robot from way back in the eighteenth century.

Here are the cams!

You've chosen to read this book so we already know you are pretty **clever** – which is why, about now, you'll be thinking to yourself . . .

All of that cam stuff is fine but what powered these early robots, if they didn't have electricity or batteries or cheese?

They probably did have cheese, but as that has nothing to do with robots we'll say no more about it and move on.

Automatons like The Writer ran on **clockwork**, like a watch or a mechanical egg timer.

Clockwork. How does a clock work?

Give us a minute. This may take some time.

You need to put **energy** in it, so you need to **wind it up**.

Call it some names or give a slow handclap?

Or you could just wind up the main spring. This tightens the spring, and energy is then stored in the wound spring. It stays wound up because of a ratchet that stops it from going in reverse. You release the energy bit by bit as the ratchet steadily moves.

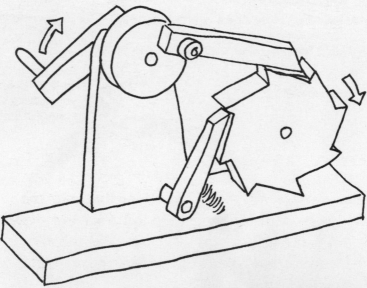

The wheel can only turn clockwise when the handle is turned – the ratchet stops it going the other way.

A clock mechanism

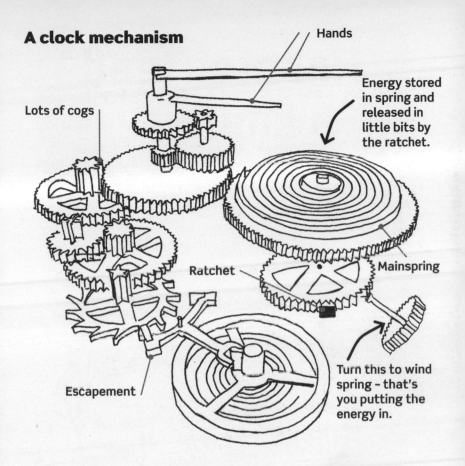

Hands

Energy stored in spring and released in little bits by the ratchet.

Lots of cogs

Mainspring

Ratchet

Escapement

Turn this to wind spring - that's you putting the energy in.

The energy is then transferred into the gears. How fast or slow the movement goes depends on the size of the gear. The gears then connect to a mechanism that makes something move - the hands in a clock or the moving parts in an automaton, for example, like the camshaft in The Writer.

Robots Need Energy

The automatons used clockwork, and modern robots use electricity, but they do the same thing: they give the robot or automaton **energy**.

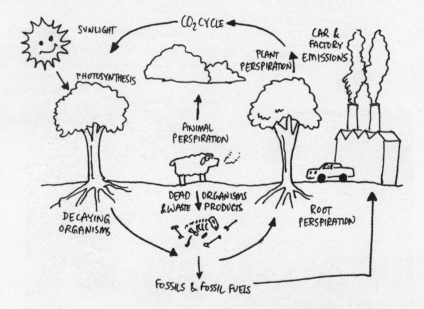

Remember, energy can't be created or destroyed. It can only be transferred from one form into another.

Both clockwork and electric robots store energy. This is the **potential energy** which can then transfer into **kinetic** or **movement energy**.

Humans need energy too . . .

Humans get energy from **food**. Food has chemical energy stored in it which originally came from the sun.

Are humans just organic robots or are robots just mechanical humans?

They both need energy to do stuff.

There is a robot called EcoBot II designed by Bristol Robotics Laboratory that was designed to get its energy from dead flies, which it would then break down and convert into electricity. It actually worked – it ran for twelve days in a row on eight houseflies.

The temperature sensor

These are blue batteries where the dead flies go.

Light sensors

EXPERIMENTS

Make this:
rolling tin

You'll need: A small cardboard tube container with a plastic lid – it could have held gravy granules or crisps
Scissors
Tape
A thick elastic band
Three thick screws

How to do it

1. Make a hole in the bottom of the container and in the lid. Push the elastic through the hole in the container so that a little loop pokes through to the outside.

2. Slip a screw through this loop and tape it in place, so the band can't slip back into the container.

3. Use a little tape to attach a screw to the middle of the elastic band inside the container.

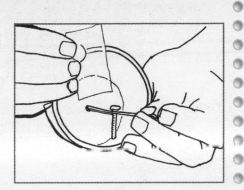

4. Push the other end of the band through the hole in the lid. Secure it with the final screw and a piece of tape, and put the lid on the container.

5. Push the container and watch it roll back again.

How does it work?

The energy from pushing the tin is transferred into the elastic band by the rolling of the tin. When the tin stops, the elastic band releases that energy as movement, and the tin rolls back in the opposite direction.

Historical Robots

We've looked at how automatons, the original mechanical robots, worked but we should also look at how the automatons started out and how they developed into the robots we know and love today.

3500 BC - A really, really long time ago. There are Greek myths of intelligent mechanical objects. The 'myths' part is quite important: it might be made up.

2500 BC - The BC years are weird: they go backwards towards zero. In Egypt they have the idea of a machine that can think.

1400 BC - A water clock thought to be one of the first robot-like devices was made in Babylonia (present-day southern Iraq).

800 BC - Greek writer Homer (not Simpson) writes about 'Golden Servants', metal beings a bit like an early robot.

350 BC - Greek mathematician Archytas of Tarentum builds a mechanical bird called - get ready for this - 'the pigeon'. It's not a great name, is it?

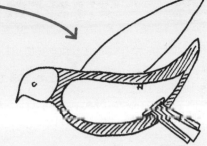

200 BC - A mechanical orchestra is built in China.

100 AD - Hero of Alexandria (that's his name, he wasn't just a brave person) wrote about theatrical automatons. He designed this wind-powered organ for theatrical sound effects.

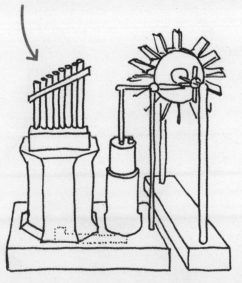

1200 - Arabian genius Al-Jazari wrote a book all about automatons.

1495 - Leonardo da Vinci's Mechanical Knight was designed.

1500s - Loads happened. In Germany, Johannes Muller von Konigsberg built a fly made of iron, and a wooden mechanical monk was also built. In Britain, John Dee built a wooden beetle that could fly.

Any chance of a bit more detail?

OK, here's an in-depth look at some really good automatons, starting with an automaton that looks a lot like the humanoid robots we see today, yet it was made in 1495.

Da Vinci's Mechanical Knight

Let's take a quick step back in time to have a look at the great **Leonardo da Vinci**, painter and decorator . . . sorry, I meant inventor. He is famous for the Mona Lisa, the Vitruvian Man and designs for early inventions like a flying machine and a parachute (which was probably in case the flying machine stopped working mid-flight). He also designed a mechanical knight.

Da Vinci's actual name was Leonardo di ser Piero Vinci. Di Vinci means from Vinci, which is a town near Florence in Italy. He was born in 1452. Young Leonardo became an apprentice to the painter Andrea del Verrocchio, which must have been when he honed his artistic skills. But Leonardo wasn't just about art; he was also an inventor of all manner of things, including tanks and underwater breathing apparatus.

Leonardo went to work in Milan where he produced one of his most famous works, *The Last Supper*. When Milan was invaded by the French in 1499 Leonardo headed to Venice, where he designed ways to defend the city against attack, like barricades which could easily be moved to defend the city. However, many of these inventions didn't make it past the design stage and never actually got built.

Leonardo headed back to Milan via Florence, and towards the end of his life he worked for the King of France, Francis I, who commissioned Leonardo to make a mechanical lion for him. But we're not sure if it got built before Leonardo died in Amboise, France, in 1519.

The Mechanical Knight was one of his inventions, and here's what you need to know about it.

The sketches for it were rediscovered in the 1950s. We're not completely sure if it was built or not but it may have been on display in Milan in 1495.

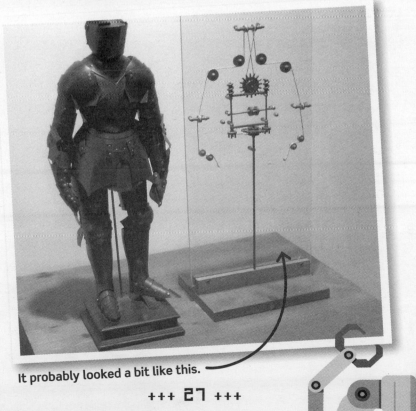

It probably looked a bit like this.

It could raise its visor to show there wasn't a human underneath which must have been a bit spooky. It could sit, stand, and make cakes – well, maybe not the last one.

It was a good knight! **Good knight**, get it? Like 'Goodnight'!

Automatons can be animals too

This one is truly incredible. It's a **swan** that swims on water and eats fish.

Built in Britain around 1773 by **John Joseph Merlin** (like the wizard, but not) and James Cox.

It toured the world and astounded audiences, so much so that the famous author Mark Twain wrote that the swan **'had a living grace about his movement and a living intelligence in his eyes'**.

So it must have been pretty realistic.

The stream is made up of rotating glass rods. The swan ducks ... sorry too many aquatic birds ... the swan can move its head down to the water, pick up a silver fish and eat it. Well, appears to eat it at least. It doesn't actually eat it because it's an automaton and unlike a real swan it doesn't need food.

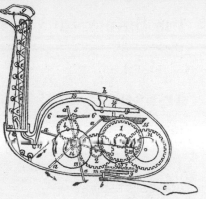

All of this is programmed in, using cogs – just like the writing boy we saw earlier.

The Automaton Chess Player

Some automatons were so clever that they were almost too clever. Yes, that's right: this one was programmed to play chess, and actually **beat** humans. It looked like this.

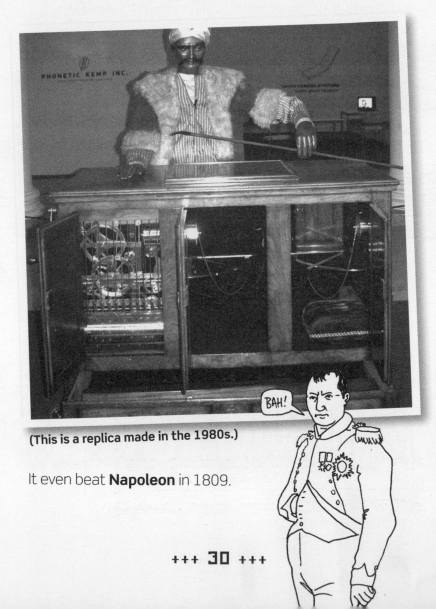

(This is a replica made in the 1980s.)

It even beat **Napoleon** in 1809.

BAH!

It was built in 1770 by Wolfgang von Kempelen.

The challenge was simple: **Beat the automaton at chess**. Pretty straightforward, you'd think. Except nobody could beat the automaton – it was too good to be true. And there was a reason for that. It wasn't true. It was a **fake**.

They'd just made a box with a person in it and put a chessboard on top. OK, it did have a clever mechanism to allow them to move the player's arm, and the chess pieces, from underneath.

What a cheat!

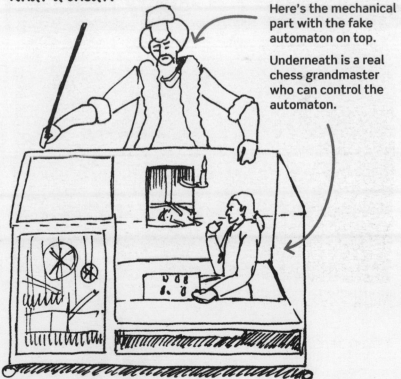

Here's the mechanical part with the fake automaton on top.

Underneath is a real chess grandmaster who can control the automaton.

It toured the world beating people at chess. All those people thought they were being beaten by a robot, but all the while it was actually a human winning the games.

This shows that automatons were so important that their inventors were prepared to go to great lengths to con people into thinking that they had made the next great technological innovation when in fact they hadn't. They'd just made a box with a person in it and put a chessboard on top.

Can you spot which of these are fake automatons?

A monk made out of wood? Is this a fake?

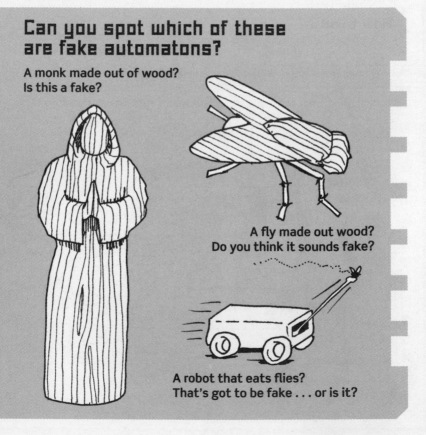

A fly made out wood? Do you think it sounds fake?

A robot that eats flies? That's got to be fake . . . or is it?

EXPERIMENTS

Make this:
a cardboard automaton

You'll need: A small cardboard box

Scissors

Tape

Dowel rods or wooden kebab skewers

Stuff to decorate it with

How to do it:

1. Cut open the front of the box. Don't throw that bit away.

2. Use that bit of cardboard to make 2 cams.

3. Carefully poke your skewer through the box and the cam.

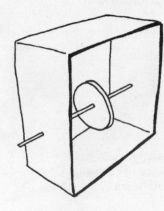

4. Take the second skewer and cam and poke them through the top of the box, so the cams touch.

Glue a short piece of straw to support the top cam.

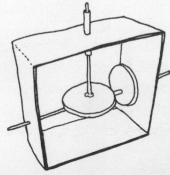

5. Turn the horizontal cam to see if it spins the vertical one. If it doesn't, tinker with it until it does.

6. Decorate the top of the skewer sticking out of the box.

Make a handle from a piece of card and another short skewer.

You could make it look like a spinning dancer, or an animal. Or you could print off a picture of a grown-up and stick their faces on the skewer. Then you'd be in control of them and they'd be your robot automaton forever . . . **ha ha ha, evil laugh, evil laugh . . .** Or not, it's up to you.

Meanwhile in other robot-related developments . . .

While automatons were being developed step-by-step from mechanical to electronic machines, there was quite a lot of other work going on, not involving automatons, that helped to develop modern robots. These developments were less about the physical aspects of a robot and more about giving our robots a **brain**.

How do you give a robot a brain?

Well, it depends on what you mean by a brain. If you want something like a human brain then there's still work to be done, but if you want a simpler brain, by which I mean a brain that can process tasks so that when you tell the robot to do something it can then do that thing, we are already there.

But how did we get there?

In order to get a robot to do something it needs to be programmed in some way. Robots don't just do things because they feel like it – because they don't have feelings unless they've been programmed to *have* feelings.

Stop! Were going round in circles. Start again.

Earlier on we looked at cams and how placing them in the right order made an automaton do things. That is an example of early **programming**.

What is Programming?

Here's what you need to know. Firstly, if you think computers and robots are clever then you are wrong. Well, you're also right, but really you are a bit wrong, so also a bit right. They *are* clever. But they do need to be told what to do and how to do it, and you do that by using programming.

To understand the stuff they are being told to do, the robots need to be told about that stuff first – a bit like when you get taught stuff at school. With robots you need to tell them about all that stuff bit by bit, in a specific order, otherwise they'd get confused – and that's programming.

Computer programming can also be called **software**.

So how do you tell your computer to do something? You can't just talk to it.

You do it by writing an **algorithm**.

An algorithm is a set of instructions that lead to an end result.

For example, when you bake a cake the recipe is an algorithm and your end result is the cake.

Getting dressed is also an algorithm: you have to put on your clothes in the correct order and in the right place, otherwise you end up with your coat on your legs and your pants on your head.

But where do algorithms come from?

'Algorithm' just sounds like an invented mathematical word but in fact 'algorithm' was actually someone's name. That person was **Al-Khwarizmi**.

Al-Khwarizmi was a Persian mathematician, astronomer and all-round clever person. He lived from 780 to 850. Persia is now modern day Iran but in Al-Khwarizmi's time it was part of the mighty Persian Empire.

Al-Khwarizmi was a scholar in the 'House of Wisdom' in Baghdad (which is now in Iraq). He worked on Algebra,

Arithmetic, Trigonometry, Geography and Algorithms.

So how did we get the word algorithm from Al-Khwarizmi?

It's all down to translation. It was probably the Romans that took his name, changed it around a bit to make it more Roman, and it stuck. So really it's Al-Khwarizmis that are the instructions that tell robots what to do, and not algorithms.

Make your own algorithm

Algorithms are easy to make. They are just a set of instructions. But **can you write one?** It could be anything from a recipe, to directions of how you get from home to the local park.

Or it could be detailed instructions of how to pick your nose . . . actually no, that's pretty disgusting and no one really needs to know that.

Write your algorithm here

Which of these can be programmed?

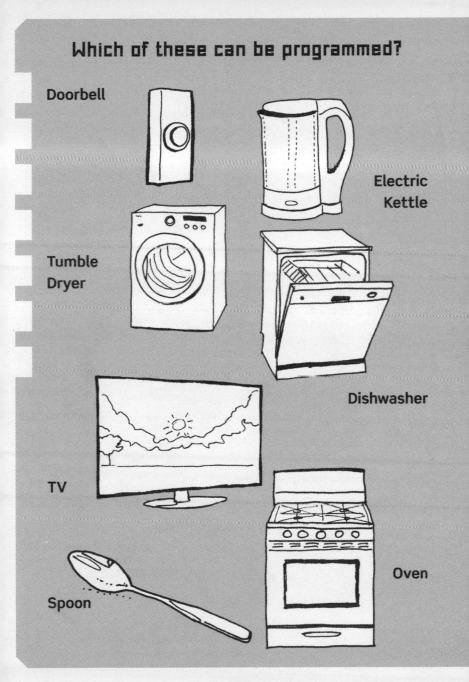

Doorbell

Electric Kettle

Tumble Dryer

Dishwasher

TV

Spoon

Oven

For automatons, using cams was a good way to store their programming, but a better way might have been to use a piece of **card**. Yes, you read that correctly: you can program a complicated piece of machinery using a bit of cardboard. Well, not just a bit. Quite a few bits, all joined together. There is a bit more to it than it seems, so don't get a bit of an old cereal packet and try to stuff it in a robot. It probably won't work and might upset the robot.

The cards were actually chains of cards with holes punched in them like this.

Punched card machines had been around for a while, but it wasn't until 1801 and the invention of the **Jacquard loom**, that they really came into their own.

A loom is a large piece of machinery used to weave material. It was much quicker using a loom than weaving by hand, though it still took time to manually set up a loom. **Joseph Marie Jacquard** sped the process up by inventing the Jacquard loom (yes, that's right, he named his invention after himself). It was designed to read punched cards which programmed the loom to adjust automatically to create beautiful patterns in the material it was weaving.

This fabric was woven on the Jacquard loom.

Here's how it works

The card has holes punched in it in particular places. The card moves through the machine. As it does, when the machine comes across a hole in the card, it moves a hook on the loom, and that hook moves and threads the pattern.

It looked like this. By changing the position of the holes on the card you could create lots of patterns accurately lots of times.

This form of programming was so good that punch card systems were still in use in computing in the 1980s.

And if you've heard of the programming term **'debugging'**, that comes from actual bugs and insects getting on the punched cards and messing things up.

So what has this got to do with robots?

Quite a lot. Like I said earlier, programming is really important for robots. Without it, robots wouldn't know what to do. It would be as if you had never gone to school.

So where do punched cards lead us to?

They lead us to **Charles Babbage**, a mathematician, inventor and engineer. That's right, he had three jobs – which seems a bit greedy.

Charles Babbage was born in London in 1791. He was quite well off as his father was a wealthy banker. Charles was an excellent mathematician as a boy and went on to study at Cambridge University.

In 1816 Charles became a fellow of the Royal Society which is like a prestigious club for all the best scientists. In 1827 Charles inherited his dad's fortune which in today's money would be worth around £8 million.

Why did Babbage design the first computer?

Charles liked things to be accurate and that was difficult to achieve all the time if all the calculations that needed to be done were done by humans who are prone to making mistakes. The British government agreed and gave him money to develop his machines.

Some people call him **'the father of the computer'** but he didn't have little computer babies that he looked after. What they meant was that Charles Babbage invented the first mechanical computer. Yes, we've had mechanical robots, now it's mechanical computers, and both of them have helped bring us the modern robots we know today.

Like Jacquard and his loom, Babbage wanted to make things easier, like using a machine to make complicated calculations quickly and accurately.

What's the difference?

The **Difference Engine**, that is. Babbage designed it back in 1822. It was pretty big – about 2.4m tall, weighing 13,600kg, with around 25,000 parts.

The new improved version, designed by Babbage around twenty years later, was the **Difference Engine No. 2**. Not a great name, a bit number two, if you don't mind.

It was like a big calculator that you could do several complicated calculations with.

The problem with it was that it was never fully built. It was thought of as too expensive. In fact Joseph Clement, who was in charge of constructing the Difference Engine, said to Babbage that he would not carry on working unless he was paid in advance. Unfortunately, there was no cash to do that – so in 1833 the project closed down.

Hang on, though. Never say never – because the Science Museum in London did build one in 1991, and even got it working.

The Difference Engine is made up of columns that represent numbers. Each column represents a number with 50 decimal places and the machine uses these to make its calculations.

The Analytical Engine

But Babbage didn't give up. Instead, he moved on to his next project, the **Analytical Engine**.

This was a mechanical computer – yes, a **mechanical computer**. A mechanical computer is to an electronic computer what a mechanical robot is to an electronic robot. It works using levers, cams and gears rather than electronics like a modern computer does. It was different to the Difference Engine because it could do more and had more functions, not unlike the computers of today.

The Analytical Engine was better and more sophisticated than the Difference Engine. It could be programmed using punched cards like the Jacquard loom. It was like an early super computer (OK, it didn't have a lot of competition at the time) and was capable of doing any calculation.

It's made of several parts. The **mill** is where the calculation is done. It's like the brain of the machine. The **store** is, as the name suggests, where the memory is stored. It's a bit like how data is stored in a modern computer. It also has the **reader** where the punchcards are read and the **printer** where all the results of the calculations are printed out.

Charles Babbage only managed to build a trial model of part of his Analytical Engine.

The **Analytical Engine** could be programmed using punched cards.

A punched card goes into the machine and little prongs poke into the holes in the punched card. However, the number you want to program in doesn't have a hole.

Let's say your number is 5. There's a hole on either side at numbers 4 and 6 but no hole at 5. The prong detects that there isn't a hole and that tells the Analytical Engine that the number being programmed is 5. This happens many, many times with lots of numbers so that tons of calculations can be done.

These are the cards Babbage used for putting in instructions.

The Analytical Engine was still being built and tested when Babbage died. This is the print mechanism for showing results.

Expense was a real problem for Babbage. His machines cost serious money to build. In fact it was estimated to cost about the same as building a ship for the navy and, because of that, the British government cut his funding and probably used the money to build a ship or something.

But Babbage continued working and designing 'engines'. It was a complicated business and he needed help with it and that help came from **Ada Lovelace**.

We don't know if she did love lace . . . maybe she didn't even like it.

Ada Lovelace

Like a modern computer, the Analytical Engine needed to be programmed, and Ada Lovelace helped with that.

Ada was the daughter of the poet Lord Byron and she was born in London in 1815. Byron left a month after Ada was born and was never to see her again, dying when she was just eight years old.

Ada's mother, Anne Isabella Milbanke, Lady Wentworth, never forgave Byron and wanted to make sure that Ada never became like him. She thought the best way not be a wild poetic type was through maths. So, Ada studied maths and studied it hard and really enjoyed it.

Later on, Ada met Charles Babbage through her tutor **Mary Somerville**. Mary Somerville was also an excellent mathematician. Somerville and astronomer Caroline Herschel were the first women to be made honorary members of the Royal Astronomical Society.

Mary knew Babbage and introduced him to Ada. Babbage called Ada the 'Enchantress of Numbers' – not because she was a magician, but because she was really good at maths.

Ada worked with Babbage and was able to explain how the Analytical Engine worked; it had most people pretty stumped at the time.

Ada wrote a detailed set of notes which she called 'Notes'. Not a great name, but she was concentrating on her maths rather than the title. She also wrote a song which she called . . . 'Song'. That's not exactly true.

Anyway, the 'Notes' are important because they include the first computer program.

Who knows what else she could have achieved if she hadn't died at the relatively young age of just thirty-six.

Ada Lovelace is a true legend of computer programming.

Talking to Computers

Instead of having to punch hundreds of cards to write programming, we can now use a computer – but you have to use a language that the computer can understand. Yes, that's right: robots need a **language** to get their instructions.

Can you guess what that language is?

It's not French . . .

It's not German . . .

It's not Chinese . . .

It's not Urdu . . .

It's not Finnish . . .

But that's the finish of that. There are actually quite a few different computer languages.

Here are just a few:

C – Yes, it's just called 'C', invented back in 1972

Python – No, not a snake, but a computer language from 1989.

Ruby – Not the precious stone. It's a precious computer language.

Java – This is the most popular one, invented in 1991.

Scratch – This is one you read about earlier. It was invented in 2002.

Why do we have so many different types? We use different types of computer language to do different tasks, as each one has its strengths and weaknesses.

Brilliant Binary

All of these languages translate into **binary code**. We use them to make programming in binary code faster. These languages create shortcuts to using binary. If we didn't use them it would take ages to program computers.

So where does 'binary' come into this and what is it?

All of these computer languages are made up of binary code.

Binary code itself is made up of **'1's** and **'0's**.

Modern binary was created by Gottfried Leibniz in 1679, but there had been older versions used by ancient Egyptians, Chinese and Indians. He worked out that you can do any calculation with them.

These 1s and 0s represent numbers and words. Which looks a bit like this:

H = 01001000
E = 01000101
L = 01001100
L = 01001100
O = 01001111

Why do we use 1s and 0s?

Computer circuits are made up of tiny switches that work by being either **on** or **off**. The best way to tell them if they need to be on or off is by using a language that only deals with on or off, and that language is binary. 1 is on, 0 is off –

that's all you need to know.

Imagine that a robot is full of little electrical circuits like light switches – each time one is clicked on or off in the correct order, the robot knows that it needs to do something.

An electrical circuit looks like this.

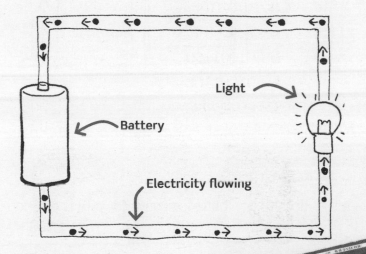

Light

Battery

Electricity flowing

Computers and robots are made up of circuits that have a sequence of **gates** that are either on or off. Gates are like very small light switches and are what make up circuit boards like this:

By programming your computer or robot, you are telling the gates to be either open or shut, and this is how the computer knows what to do.

Think of it like this:

I want the robot to say **'hello'** so I have to write the code to do this. I put it into binary for the robot so all those 1's and 0's will come out as 'Hello'.

Or to put it another way, you might want your robot to move forward, so you'll input **'move forward'**. This is then translated into a programming language like Java or Python and that is then translated into binary code. This code will instruct the circuits, or gates, to switch on and off in the correct sequence, and that sequence tells the robot to move forward.

Famous Robots

We've explored how robots came about through a combination of building fantastic machines that appear to be alive, and clever programming – the brains behind a robot, which allows us to give a robot instructions, and enables the robot to follow those instructions. **But why are we so fascinated by robots?**

Is it because they appear to be alive and, even though we know they aren't, we want to believe they are and see what incredible things they can do? Or is it that we see them as fun toys to entertain us? Perhaps it's because humans like creating and building things, and we all like to see if we can do a better job than nature can?

Whatever the reason, robots have a lot of fans, and to many of them it doesn't seem to matter if the robots are real or if they only exist in books or films.

The term **'robot'** started in the theatre and robots have continued to be popular in science-fiction films and books. Overleaf are a few of the best ones. These are all fictional robots, but they did inspire a lot of robots that we have today, which proves it's always worth imagining stuff because it might come in handy later on.

Tik-Tok from the book *Ozma of Oz*, which is one of The Wizard of Oz books. Tik-Tok is a big copper ball with arms, legs and a head. A bit like an automaton, Tik-Tok needed winding up.

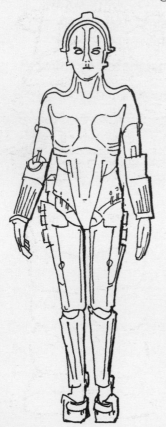

Maria from the 1927 Fritz Lang film *Metropolis*. This is an iconic robot that we still see lots of images of today. She even looks a bit like a robot from a very popular series of films set in space featuring a robot. Know which one? C-3PO in *Star Wars*. In fact it's said that C-3PO is actually a male version of Maria.

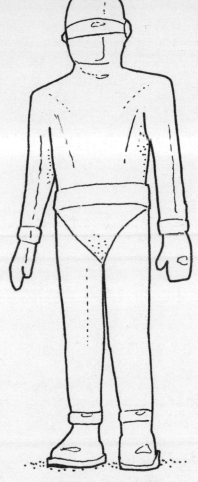

Gort from the film *The Day the Earth Stood Still*, originally made in 1951 – but another version was made in 2008. Gort is a very famous robot but a bit more menacing than some of the others.

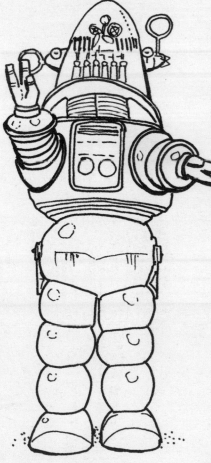

Robby the Robot from the 1956 film *Forbidden Planet*. Did you know this was based on William Shakespeare's play *The Tempest*?

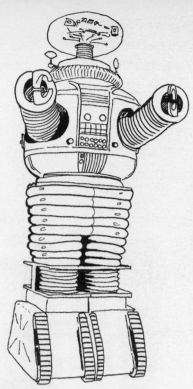

The **Robot** from *Lost in Space* (a 1960's TV show and later a 1998 film). Hmm, not really working too hard on the name here . . .

K-9 was a robot dog that helped the Doctor battle aliens in *Doctor Who*.

C 3PO, **R2-D2**, **BB-8** – the robots from the *Star Wars* films have got to be the most famous of them all.

A Great Leap Forward

The next real leap for robots was using **electricity** to power them. Nowadays we can get hold of a quick recharge for anything from a phone to a car, but it used to be much more difficult to access electricity. It wasn't until the twentieth century that electricity was more easily available, and it's in the twentieth century that robots start to look more like, well . . . robots.

What makes these new robots different?

Instead of cams and cogs, like the automatons we looked at before, they are using circuits and electricity to work. They tended to be made of metal and look a bit more like what you'd draw if someone said to you **'Draw a robot'**.

In fact, why don't you draw a robot right now?

You probably drew something that looked like a metal human. If not, well done! You're very creative. Robots that look like humans are very popular and are often referred to as 'humanoid' robots (because they look a bit like humans). However, they weren't all like that.

My Robot

Introducing Elmer and Elsie – tortoise robots!

Elmer and Elsie were built by William Grey Walter between 1948 and 1949. They don't look like humans at all. In fact a lot of people thought they looked like **tortoises**.

William Grey Walter was born in the USA in 1910 but later moved to the UK to study and ended up staying.

William was obsessed with brains (no, he wasn't a zombie) and wanted to show how they worked by making a robot.

But not any old robot. These were robots that could respond to light like a living creature might. The robots used the light to find recharging points when they ran low on battery power. This was done to simulate how a very tiny part of the brains of living things might work. For example, humans recharge by eating and sleeping. You might be recharging right now while you're reading this book—hopefully by eating, not by falling asleep.

Did I mention that they looked like tortoises?

Unlike actual tortoises, these robots ran on three wheels. Real tortoises only do that if they are riding tricycles.

Elmer and Elsie are important because their design has inspired and influenced the robots of today.

Quite a lot of robots
did look like humans,
though. Like Eric.

Eric the Robot

Eric was first built in
1928.

He could **stand up**.

He could **talk**.

He was made of
aluminium.

He was **Superman** . . .
No he wasn't. He was
a robot.

He was the UK's first
robot.

He had lightbulbs for
eyes.

He weighed 45kg.

He was built by Captain William H. Richards and Alan
Reffell. The pair were veterans of the First World War.
William was a war correspondent (that's a journalist, not
someone who writes letters to wars) and Alan was an
aircraft mechanic in the Royal Flying Corps (this later
became the RAF).

Why did they build Eric?

It was all thanks to the Duke of York's busy schedule. William had asked the Duke to attend the Society of Model Engineers annual exhibition but he couldn't make it, so William decided they needed a substitute, so they built one. The substitute was to be a mechanical man called 'Eric'.

A robot opening an exhibition was big news, and Eric became a bit of a star and toured the world, with people coming from far and wide to see him.

But then Eric disappeared.

Sometime in the 1930s Eric went missing and no one knows where he went.

Maybe Eric was so sophisticated that he simply walked off and started a new life. Maybe he got a job as a waiter.

But don't worry. Eric has been rebuilt, thanks to a crowd-sourcing project where lots of people got together so that the Science Museum in London could bring Eric back to life.

Gakutensoku

This is the first Japanese robot. It was built just a year after Eric, in Osaka, Japan, in 1929 by Makota Nishimura.

'Gakutensoku' means 'learning from the laws of nature'.

Gakutensoku moved with a mechanism using air pressure.

Air-pressure mechanisms work by increasing pressure on the air, which makes the air push harder against an object, making the object move – in this case making parts of the robot move.

EXPERIMENTS
Air Pressure

You can do an experiment with air pressure to demonstrate how useful it is.

You'll need: A glass of water (about a third full)
A card – it could be playing card, but it must fit entirely over the top of the glass.

How to do it:

1. Put the card on top of the glass of water.

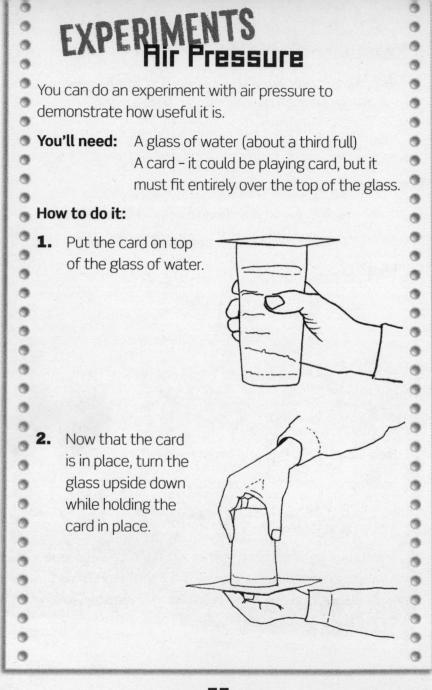

2. Now that the card is in place, turn the glass upside down while holding the card in place.

3. Now take your hand away. The card stays in place and no water falls out.

Why?

Because the **air pressure** is different on each side of the card. The pressure pushing **up** is higher than the pressure pushing **down**.

That's why it's a force. It's no pushover!

How does this make a robot move?

Think of air pressure as being the weight of air. Yes, that's right: air has weight because it's a thing – it's made up of gases.

If you squash air it'll try to escape, but if it can't escape it will push things out of its way. In a robot built to use air pressure, the air is squashed to move a piston which then moves a part of the robot.

Elektro the Moto-Man

Yes, it *is* a good name, but it gets better. He had a robot dog called **Sparko**.

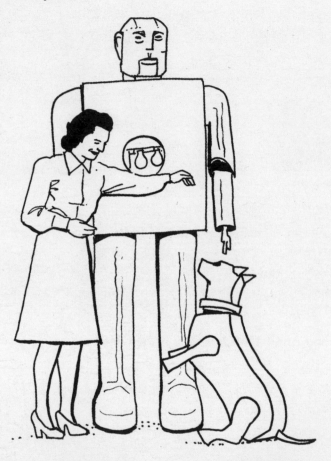

Elektro was built in Mansfield, Ohio, USA between 1937 and 1938 by the Westinghouse Electric Corporation.

Elektro weighed 120.2kg.

Elektro was 2.1m tall.

Elektro could speak **700 words** using a record player. A **record player** is an old way of playing music. A record is a disc that has a sound recording on it. To hear the sound on the disc it's put on a record player and made to start spinning at the right speed. Then a needle is lowered on to it, which then transfers the information stored on the disc and converts it back into sound. Then sound is played through a speaker so that the listener can hear it.

Elektro was made of aluminium.

His eyes could tell the difference between green and red light. Lovely if he went driving and came to some traffic lights . . .

BUT WHAT'S THAT COLOUR IN BETWEEN RED AND GREEN?

Need a **balloon** blown up? Elektro could do it.

Sparko the robot dog could do anything a real dog could do . . . as long as all you wanted a real dog to do was bark, sit and beg.

George – the first Transformer?

Maybe . . . because
George was originally
a Wellington bomber plane.

However, **George** didn't exactly transform from a plane
into a robot. George was built by Tony Sale in 1949 from
scrap metal *salvaged* from a Wellington bomber. Tony
was an electronic engineer, computer programmer and a
curator at the Science Museum. He built robots as a child
and went on building them as an adult and that's how
George came about.

George was 1.83m (6ft) tall and is the only one of his kind.

George ran on two motorcycle batteries.

BUT WHY DID THEY TAKE BOTH BATTERIES?

George was built of **aluminium** and **duralumin**.

Aluminium is a metal that is strong, light and doesn't rust like iron does.

Duralumin is made of aluminium, copper, manganese and magnesium.

George cost only £15 to make, which would be around £350 today.

Ciao, Cygan!

Almost a decade later it's 1957 and we've got **Cygan**.

He's kind of got a punk hairdo going on, but this robot is some serious business.

Cygan was built by Dr Pietro Fiorito in Turin, Italy.

It was 2.4m tall and weighed 453kg.

It ran on a 28-volt battery for up to 4.5 hours.

It had 170 valves—

What's a valve?

A valve looks like this.

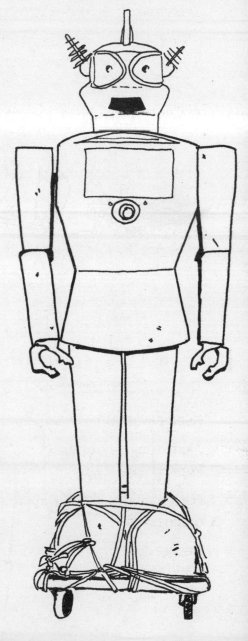

Valves were used in early electronic items like radios to control electric current between electrodes.

Cygan could move three metres a minute, which is really slow.

It could go in all directions – forward, back, left, right. Not up or down, though . . . so not really *all* directions.

How was Cygan operated?

Some people reported that it was voice-controlled but this seems rather unlikely. It was probably by remote control, meaning someone was controlling it.

MAKE ME A SANDWICH, CYGAN!

I CAN'T. THE LADY WHO CONTROLS ME HAS GONE FOR LUNCH...

Robot Laws

At the same time that these robots were being built, we had started to think about what robots could do for humans and how we wanted them to act. It turns out that we wanted them to act mainly as servants that could do the jobs that we couldn't be bothered to do.

But is that such a bad thing if it frees up your time to create the next batch of robots?

If you think about it though, the more intelligent we make robots, the more likely it becomes that they won't want to do our jobs and they might even get angry if they're told to do things they don't want to do.

This is why people like acclaimed science-fiction author and biochemist Isaac Asimov wrote the three laws of robotics. (He also first used the term 'robotics'.)

What are the three laws of robotics?

They are something that Asimov first wrote in the science-fiction story *Runaround*, but because they made so much sense they've been adopted by the world of science fact.

Here they are:

1. Always brush your teeth before bed.

Wait a minute, that's not right. Do robots even have teeth and, if they do, would they need to brush them because they probably wouldn't eat food either so the teeth wouldn't get dirty, or would they?

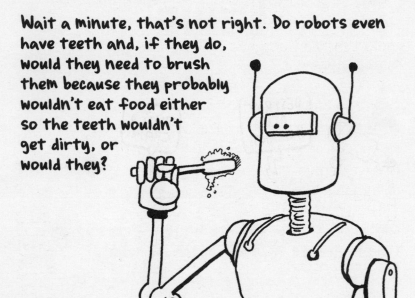

Here are the actual three laws of robotics:

1. A robot may not injure a human being or, through inaction, allow a human being to come to harm.

2. A robot must obey the orders given it by human beings, except where such orders would conflict the first law.

3. A robot must protect its own existence as long as such protection does not conflict with the first and second law.

Seems fair enough to keep your robot-self alive unless that means you have to crush some people to do that.

This is all good stuff, but your robot has to be sophisticated to be able to have all that programmed into it so it can recognize what humans are and what humans aren't.

Asimov also wrote a fourth law, which was meant as a bit of joke.

4. For every expert there is an equal and opposite expert.

It's not a side-splitter but he probably means that people tend to think they are always right.

Alan Turing

Alan Turing is important to the history of robots because he was a pioneer of computer science and artificial intelligence.

Alan Turing was born in London in 1912. At school he did really well at science and maths. In fact he wanted to go to school so much that during the General Strike of 1926, when all public transport was cancelled, he cycled sixty miles to get there.

Alan Turing worked as a code beaker during the Second World War. He helped break the **Enigma** code. The Enigma code was a highly sophisticated way of communicating used by the German military.

How did it work?

First you need an **Enigma machine**.

Then you type in your message on the **keyboard**: **'HELLO'**.

As you press each key, inside the Enigma machine a letter lights up on the lightboard to show which letter will replace it. A current travels around a complicated circuit of wiring on three wheels, or **rotors**. The rotors move as you type, to alter the circuitry. Yes, it was already tricky. Now it's even *more* tricky to follow.

Rotors

Lightboard

Keyboard

Confusingly, the same letters might not come out the same after they are **encrypted**. ('Encryption' means putting a message into code.) So if you type the letter A, it might change to a P the first time and then when you press it again come out as a Z. That's why the Enigma code was so hard to crack.

It's very confusing and nearly impossible to unscramble the coded letters unless you managed to match the exact same setting on another machine. In which case you could run the encrypted message through and decrypt it.

So Alan Turing and his team at Bletchley worked out a way to decipher those messages using a giant machine that they had built called **'Bombe'**.

Later, he designed the Automatic Computing Engine or **ACE**.

Here's the pilot ACE which went on to influence the design of loads of computers.

Alan also came up with something that is particularly important to artificial intelligence that might be used in robots: **'The Turing Test'**.

'The Turing Test' is a test. But you could probably have guessed that. It is a test about artificial intelligence designed to see if you can tell the difference between a machine and a human body. We can try it now.

Which is a machine, which is a human?

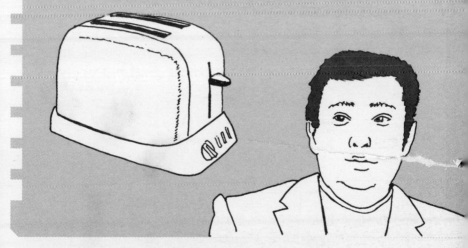

Sorry, it wasn't actually *that* easy.

Let's say for example you want a robot to act like a human: it needs to talk in a way a human does. But to make it convincing is tricky, because the robot would have to think like a human and have artificial intelligence. That's intelligence that's been programmed into the robot, not like the natural intelligence that you have.

Here's how the test works.

You need a **human** and a **machine** (we'll use a robot).

Then you need **another human** who can't see the other human and robot. We'll call them **'the questioner'**.

'The questioner' asks questions of both the human and the robot, **but** they don't know which is which.

It's all done on screens so the questioner doesn't get clues from voices.

If the questioner can't tell the difference between the human and the robot then the robot **passes the test**.

YAY!

HOORAY!

Try your own Turing Test

You can set up your own version of a Turing Test at home.

All you need is a couple of friends and a phone or tablet that can use voice recognition such as SIRI or Cortana.

Write down three questions, like, 'What's your favourite food?' or 'Where do you buy shoes from?' It doesn't matter what the questions are.

Then leave the room and get your friends to write out their answers, **but** also get them to ask the questions to the phone or tablet and write what answers it gives.

Then come back into the room and see if you can work out which are the **human answers** and which ones came from the **device**.

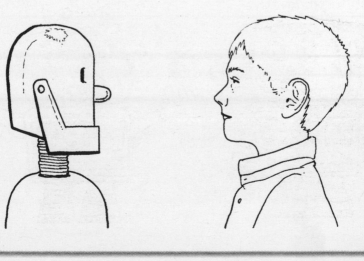

Modern Robots

Brainpower aside, robots still have a long way to go to master the things we take for granted . . . like **standing** and **walking**.

In the 1980s development started on a robot that could walk on its own. That robot was **ASIMO**.

ASIMO is probably one of the most famous robots ever.

ASIMO stands for **Advanced Step in Innovative Mobility**. You can see why they went with ASIMO. Otherwise it would take you all day to say the name.

It was first revealed by Honda in 2000.

ASIMO is 130cm tall and weighs 50kg.

Why is ASIMO so special?

Because ASIMO can walk like a human.
Which is really difficult to do (more on that later).

ASIMO can also run. Yes, run at up to 9km an hour. ASIMO can even go upstairs, which a robot needs incredible balance to do.

There have been a few advances over the years. ASIMO can now recognize people's faces and knows when to shake people's hands. Perhaps one of the most important but underrated developments is the **battery power**, which has doubled over the years, meaning the latest version can operate at full power for over an hour without needing to be charged. ASIMO can also talk in **English** and **Japanese**.

ASIMO has also toured the world demonstrating all sorts of skills, including conducting the Detroit Symphony Orchestra.

Maybe one day there might be a whole **orchestra** made up of robots.

WHAT DO WE START ON, 0 OR 1?

ASIMO isn't all about entertaining us. The aim is to develop robots that can help people, and not just with the odd job around the house, but with assisting people who are less able to get on with their lives without help.

The Robot Orchestra

If we are going to have a **Robot Orchestra** we need robots that can play instruments. In which case we need to give Toyota a call, because they've developed a humanoid robot that can play the trumpet and the violin.

Humanoid is part of a family of **Partner Robots** who are designed to assist people, even though at the moment it's all about entertainment.

I DON'T WANT TO BLOW MY OWN TRUMPET...

...BUT I CAN BLOW MY OWN TRUMPET.

Trumpet Humanoid was first built in 2005. It weighs 40g and is 1.48m tall.

How does a robot play a trumpet?

It blows air out and the robot's lips vibrate like a human's would. To operate the valves of the trumpet the robot has piston-controlled fingers.

How does a robot play the violin?

The **violin-playing humanoid** robot was built in 2007, weighs 56kg and is 1.52m tall.

The robot both holds and plays the violin like a human would.

But why?

Both robots are demonstrating how incredibly dexterous they are, showing their ability to do very finely controlled movements with their hands. They are designed to help in hospitals and around the house.

RIBA II

Here's another robot designed to help people. It's a robot that can give you a bit of a lift. Well, quite a lot of a lift, as they can actually pick you up.

This is **RIBA II**. RIBA II helps people who aren't able to get up by themselves.

RIBA stands for **Robot for Interactive Body Assistance**.

It runs on wheels and uses sensors made of rubber to make sure the process of picking the person up is as comfortable as possible.

UPSY-DAISY!

Valkyrie

This robot is all about **space**.

Valkyrie was built by NASA and is also known as the humanoid R5 robot. We'll stick with Valkyrie.

Valkyrie is 1.8m tall and weighs 125kg.

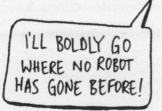

I'LL BOLDLY GO WHERE NO ROBOT HAS GONE BEFORE!

It was first built for search and rescue in disaster situations.

Valkyrie has **32 degrees** of freedom in its body, which means it is **rather flexible**. If you have a toy car that doesn't have wheels that turn left or right it only has **one degree** of freedom. The more degrees of freedom means the more directions and positions you can move in. This is useful for moving around in general.

Eventually NASA hopes to send Valkyrie to Mars.

But why send a robot to Mars?

It could be used as company for astronauts on their long journey, or it could be used instead of sending astronauts. Mars is quite a long way away so it makes sense to use robots as they don't get bored or lonely and they don't get tired or need to sleep, but most importantly it means the spaceship doesn't need to carry any oxygen or food because robots don't breathe or eat.

So, robots could be the future of space exploration. But what will those robots look like?

So you're an astronaut up in space and you're a little lonely. Is there anyone who can help?

Kirobo can.

Kirobo

Kirobo is a robot designed by the University of Tokyo and Toyota to be an astronaut's friend and keep them company. This could be really important on a long space mission in the future because we don't want astronauts getting sad and bored.

Kirobo is 34cm tall and weighs about 1kg. It's important to be light as the more equipment weighs on a space mission the more difficult it is to get the rocket up into space.

Kirobo's main design feature is to be someone an astronaut can chat to, so it is programmed to understand conversation and talk.

What else could robots help out with in space?

Well, they could be **space drones** – helicopter drones flying over the surface of planets like Mars exploring the surface much faster than the land-based rover can.

NASA is also developing a robot submarine to explore the seas of **Titan**, which is the largest of Saturn's moons.

But they won't be going under*water* because the sea isn't made of water. It's made of **liquid hydrocarbons**.

What are liquid hydrocarbons?

They are the liquid form of gases like methane (which *some* people might call fart gas) and propane C (which is used in gas barbecues).

They are liquids, not gases, because it's **really cold** on Titan.

Astronauts in space might also be able to control robots working on the surface of a planet.

Astronauts **Andreas Mogensen** and **Tim Peake** have done just that from the International Space Station.

The ISS was 400km above the earth, travelling at 7.66km per second which is 27,600km per hour. Otherwise known as **really fast**.

Mogensen controlled a robot called **'Interact Centaur'**, which has sensors built in so that the astronaut can feel what the robot feels.

The task involved placing some **pegs** in some **holes**, which is quite difficult to do if you're in space. If you're not convinced, just find a friend, go into a different room to them and shout instructions to them of how to put pegs into holes. It'll probably be quite hard.

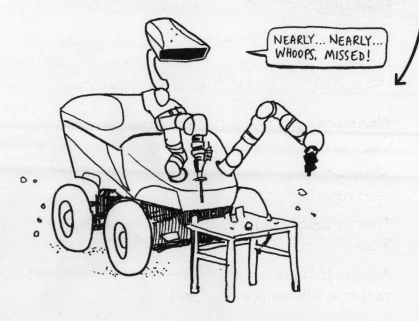

Tim Peake controlled another robot called **Bridget**.

This time the plan was to navigate the surface of **Mars**. (It wasn't Mars, though: it was a big sand pit near London.)

Hopefully, this sort of robot will be exploring the **real** surface of Mars sometime soon.

If you have a remote-control car you could set up your own Mars surface experiment by setting up various obstacles and seeing if you can control the car. To make it like a space mission, see how far away you can control it from and still be accurate.

So we've seen a robot that can help astronauts out in space. But what about a robot that can help us down here on earth?

Well, here it is: **Atlas**, a robot designed to rescue people.

Atlas. Wow. The names just get better and better. Atlas is an American robot built by Boston Dynamics.

Atlas is a search and rescue robot, built to go into places that humans cannot.

Atlas is 1.75 metres tall and weighs 82 kg.

Atlas was entered in a robotics competition and was able to complete these tasks:

1. Drive a vehicle – Oh yes, Atlas can drive!
2. Walk across rubble.
3. Remove debris.
4. Open a door and enter a building.
5. Climb a ladder.
6. Use a tool to break through a concrete pond.
7. Locate and close a valve near a leaky pipe.
8. Connect a fire hose and turn a valve on.

Atlas is a serious all-round rescue robot.

Robot Parts

The robots we've seen are good – but have you ever wondered what parts you would need to make a robot? Wonder no more, as here is almost everything you could need to build a robot.

Brains

Let's start with brains. Do robots have brains? Sort of: you could call the **CPU** their brain.

What's a CPU?

It's a bit like a robot's brain: you just read it! Seriously, CPU stands for **Central Processing Unit**.

CPU's carry out instructions.

Those instructions come from programming, and that programming is stored in the computer's memory.

It's usually done in 3 stages.

1. Fetch
The instruction to do an action has to be fetched from the memory.

2. Decode
Once the instruction has been fetched, it needs to be decoded so it can be sent to other parts of the CPU.

3. Execute (Don't worry no robots are harmed in this process.)
This is the part when the CPU carries out the instruction. So if it was to 'turn left', this is where the turning left happens.

An important part of a human brain is memory, but what's memory in a robot?

It's where the programs get stored.

RAM (or **Random Access Memory**) is the most common type of memory. The information stored in the memory can be accessed randomly, making it quicker to get to whatever's required. Using this method, you can take out the bits of information you need from wherever they are stored, instead of going through all of the memory, in a particular sequence, each time in order to find what you are after.

Memory can also be stored on a **hard drive**.

Hard drives were invented in 1954 and initially stored just 3.75 megabytes.

A **byte** is a unit of digital information. It's what computer memory is measured in. 1 byte is not very much memory. It's about the same as 1 or 2 words in an email.

1,024 bytes is 1 **kilobyte** (kb) which is about the same size as an essay you might write at school.

1,024 kilobytes is 1 **megabyte** (mb). A megabyte is about the same amount of information as this book.

1,024 megabytes is 1 **gigabyte** (gb). This is getting a bit bigger and it's about the same amount of information stored in 1,000 books.

1,024 gigabytes is a **terabyte** (tb), so we're in a library load of information now.

1,024 terabytes is a **petabyte** (pb) – this is enormous. In fact, it's enormously enormous . . . about 1,000,000,000 books, which is a **lot** of reading. However, although this may sound big, it's still probably only about **half** the memory our human brains can store.

A computer hard drive

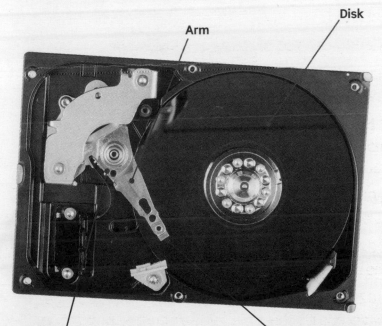

Disk

Arm

Actuator

Read/write head

Sensors

Robots need sensors to tell them what's going on around them. Robots like Elmer and Elsie had light sensors and robots today have loads of sensors.

Here's a few of them and how they work.

Cameras

They help robots to see, and the humans that may be operating the robots will use the cameras to see what's going on.

How does a robot know how close it is to an object or an obstacle?

It uses a **proximity sensor**, like an infrared one for example.

Infrared sensors work by sending out an infrared light. When the robot gets close to an object the infrared light bounces back and a receiver on the robot responds by saying there is something in the way.

Infrared – is a special type of light that we can't see, though it is there.

Ultrasonic – is used in a similar way to infrared, but instead of light it sends out sound waves which bounce back to indicate if something is in the way.

If that sounds a bit too hi-tech, how about using sensors that work simply by **touching** an object to detect it's there?

Robots can also use **sound sensors** – this could be just a microphone to detect and respond to sound.

Light sensors can detect low or high levels of light and respond accordingly. For example, if they detect low light it might send a signal to switch some lights on.

Temperature sensors simply measure temperatures. They could be useful if you're a rescue robot going into a burning building.

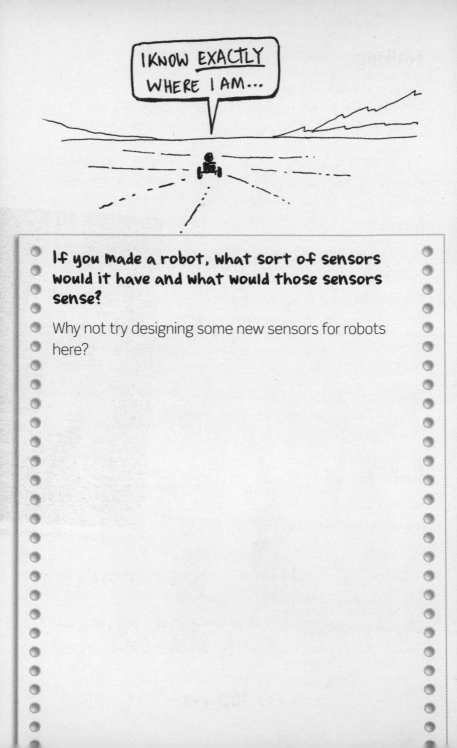

If you made a robot, what sort of sensors would it have and what would those sensors sense?

Why not try designing some new sensors for robots here?

Walking

Walking is **really hard** for robots to do well. It is something us humans take for granted but, believe it or not, it's pretty tricky to get right in a robot.

The first thing a robot needs to walk are **legs**. You could choose as many as you want but we'll go humanoid and choose **two**. This makes our robot **bipedal**.

Humans have toes, knees, hips, feet and joints which allow us to move. We also shift our weight as we walk, which is how we stay balanced.

Robots need to try to replicate all of these things to help them walk. So a walking robot has to shift its weight. It can do this by swinging its arms like a human does.

Robot legs

Robots with two legs like humans are called **bipedal**.

Human legs are difficult to replicate. A robot's legs need to deal with **actuators**, which are like the muscles in a human's legs, to move.

They also need to deal with how it shifts its weight when it walks, otherwise it will fall over. It's something humans do too without thinking about: we use our arms and the rest of our body, and robots have to do a similar thing.

Robots also need lots of **degrees of motion** - these are the parts that allow movement, like human knees and ankles do. A good robot needs six degrees of motion or more on its legs.

Robot foot

The feet are also important as the foot absorbs the impact of each step. The other thing they need to cope with are uneven surfaces, meaning robots need sensors on the bottom of their feet to detect what is underneath so it can respond accordingly and not fall over.

Wheels

Wheels are much easier to put on a robot than legs. Wheels usually make a robot faster and more stable. Lots of robot companies start by trying to make their robots walk, but when they realize just how tricky that is, they decide to put wheels on their robot instead.

The types of wheels that robots use can really vary.

You could use **two** wheels . . .

(Well, three wheels actually: two big ones and one really small one.)

Even **four** wheels or **six** wheels.

Or **track** wheels . . .

Big wheels help robots go over tough terrain.

This **Mars Rover** is a really cool robot. It's the size of a car – 2.9m long and 2.2m high. It has six 50cm wheels. The wheels help it go over Mars's rocky surface.

Robots can also be **little balls**, a bit like BB-8.
They have a motor and wheels inside the ball
that make it move.

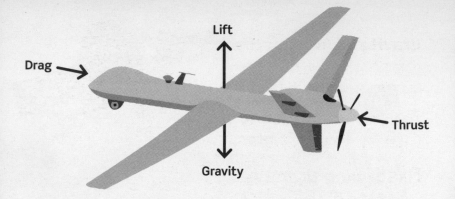

Lift

Drag →

Thrust

↓ Gravity

Flying

Flying robots are often call **drones**. Drones are really popular and could be delivering packages very soon. But how do they work?

First of all they need to deal with four things essential to flight: lift, thrust, drag and gravity.

Lift. You get lift by air flowing over a wing. The wing is an aerofoil shape which means it's got a curved top and a flatter bottom. Air moves faster over the top of the wing than under it, creating lower pressure above the wing than below it. This is what creates lift.

Thrust is created by propellers or jet engines. They push the aircraft forward, creating the airflow over the wing.

Drag slows you down when you want to go fast. Aircraft like our flying robots need to be streamlined to keep drag to a minimum.

Gravity is a force that pulls things together, in this case our flying robot to the earth.

There are two main types of drone: fixed wing and copter.

Fixed-wing drones

The first one was built in 1973 by Tadiran Electronic Industries.

They tend to be remote-controlled, using **GPS** (Global Positioning Systems).

GPS uses **satellites** to fix the position of something on earth, or in this case, near the earth.

Copter-based drones

Quadcopters use four sets of rotors to fly.

They are a bit like helicopters, but with more rotors.

The four rotors make quadcopters stable and are used for taking aerial photos and films.

They could be used for delivering packages in the very near future too.

Swimming

Robots can also be used in the water.

But how do they swim?

They can use a propeller like conventional boats, which is OK, but using **biomimetics** can be much more interesting.

Biomimetics is the method scientists use to imitate things in the natural world to solve problems.

For our robots this means copying fish to help them swim.

They have a flexible body that allows it to move from side to side so that the tail propels it through the water.

PacX Wave Glider is a robot that swam 16,668km from the USA to Australia.

It took over a year, but it did it all on its own – without the help of humans.

That's impressive, but what about a humanoid swimming robot?

Japanese researchers are building 'Swumanoid': a robot that swims like a human. It will be used for research and as a rescue robot and will be about half the size of an adult human.

DON'T WORRY, I'LL SAVE YOU!

Actuators

Actuators get robots moving. They can be electric, pneumatic or hydraulic.

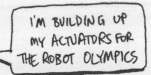

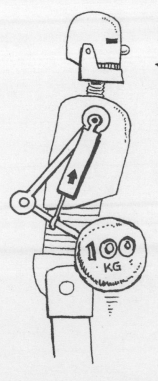

I'M BUILDING UP MY ACTUATORS FOR THE ROBOT OLYMPICS

They are kind of like muscles for a robot. Humans use muscles to help us to move ourselves, but also other things, like picking something up. We use the muscles in our legs to help us stand, and the muscles in our arms to lift and carry things. Robots use actuators in the same way: to help them stand up or pick things up.

Motors

Robots need **motors** to make them go.

Motors are found in washing machines, power drills and microwaves. They are also found in robots.

They're straightforward things, you put electricity in and it makes a metal rod turn. That metal rod might be attached to a **wheel**, or a **gear**, or the **plate** that turns around in your microwave.

Tiny little ones like this are good for small robots, like one you might make at home.

Here's how an electric motor works:

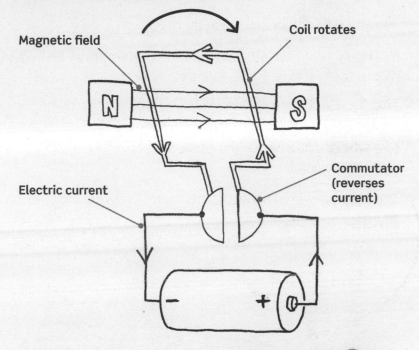

Magnetic field

Coil rotates

Commutator (reverses current)

Electric current

The bigger the robot, the more powerful the motor will need to be.

A robot like the **KUKA KR 1000** needs nine motors and could lift a ton.

We have electric motors thanks to scientists like **Michael Faraday**.

Faraday was born in London in 1791. He didn't go to school but learned through experimentation, and the guidance of another great scientist, **Humphrey Davy**. Through his experiments Faraday realized that **electricity** and **magnetism** were forms of the same thing: something he called **electromagnetism**. (See what he did there . . . ? He just mashed the words together.) This discovery led to the first electric motor.

Arms

Arms are extremely important parts of robots; in fact sometimes an entire robot can just be an arm.

There are many different types of robot arms.

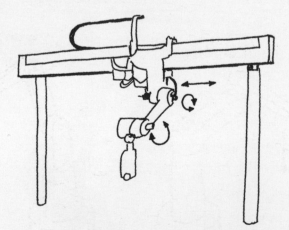

Gantry arms are designed for work on assembly lines, usually making printed circuit boards.

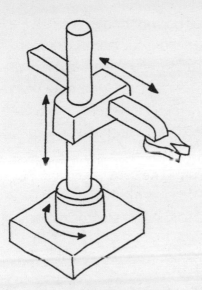

For **spot-welding**, a cylindrical robot will do the job – or a spherical robot.

For **spray-painting**, an articulated robot with three rotary joints would be handy – or should that be **army**?

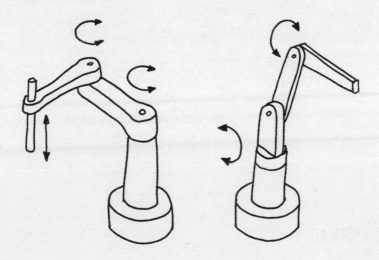

But the most famous one is the **Canadarm**.

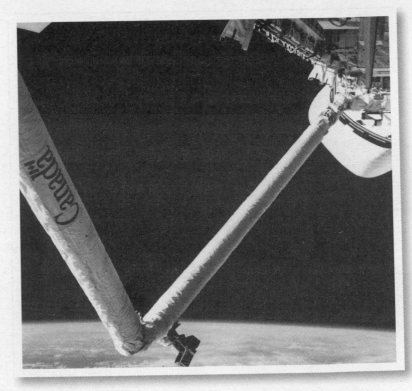

The Canadarm was first tested in space on the Space Shuttle Columbia in 1981 and nowadays an updated version is used on the **International Space Station**.

An astronaut operates it from inside the space station, and can see what's going on via cameras that are mounted outside.

It can lift up to 116,000kg and fully extended is 17.6 metres long.

Robot arms aren't only used in space, though. They are actually much more common on earth. In fact, there are **millions** in factories all across the world and they are extremely important for making things because they can do the same thing over and over again for absolutely ages. They are often used to do things that us humans would find difficult to do.

At first people didn't like the idea of robots replacing humans in factories as it meant people losing their jobs. However, over time we came to accept them as essential in the modern workplace.

Robots at the Skoda factory in the Czech Republic.

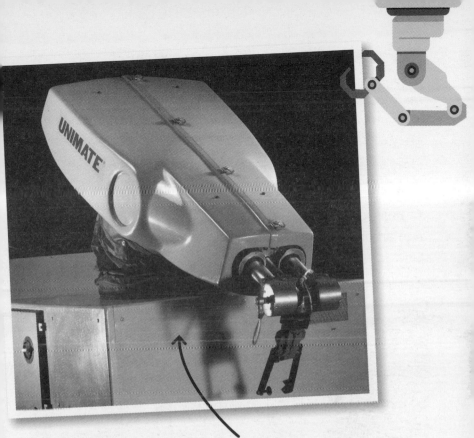

The first industrial robot was **Unimate**. It worked on an assembly line building cars for General Motors in the USA in 1961.

Unimate was very useful because it did a job that would have been dangerous for humans to do.

How long do you think a robot can work in a day?

24 hours – That's the whole day! Robots don't need light to work in either, so you can switch all the lights off in the factory which can save energy.

How do robots pick up such heavy things?

One way is by using **big springs**.

That's right: springs – the boing, boing type of springs. They sit in a cylinder (a cylinder is usually a metal tube) and inside that cylinder is a piston.

The piston moves inside the cylinder, squashing the spring, which then pushes the piston back.

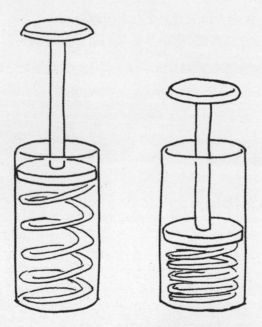

It's this motion that helps our robots lift things.

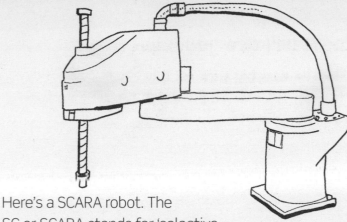

Here's a SCARA robot. The SC or SCARA stands for 'selective compliance', meaning it can only move in two planes: left and right, but not up and down.

It works because it can move easily from side to side and *quickly* – that's the main thing. Although that sounds simple it is key to a successful industrial robot.

An average industrial robot can pack **600 sweets** into boxes in a **minute**.

Beat the robot

Here's a challenge for you. Find a box of something. It doesn't have to be sweets – it could be biscuits or you could get some random objects.

Place your objects – and there needs to be quite a few of them to be challenging (at least twenty).

Then see how quickly you can pack them.

Try it a few times and see how many you can pack in a minute. **Can you beat 600?**

Dr Robot will see you now

What if the accuracy of a robot arm could be used to help humans by performing difficult surgical procedures?

Robots that can do surgery already exist. Like this one:

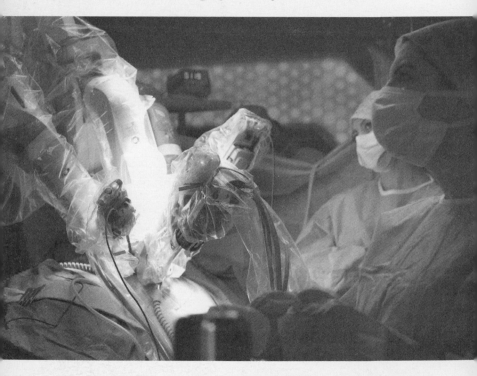

This is the **da Vinci** surgical robot. It's not autonomous as it still needs a surgeon to operate it but it does have the advantage of being super-steady, meaning it can be more precise than a human surgeon operating manually.

The first robot surgeon was **Arthrobot** in 1983.

In the future robots may be used more often to perform operations where accuracy is essential. They may also help in situations where a doctor is not available, like in a remote part of the world or on a space mission. The robot could be controlled by a doctor in another location to perform the surgery.

Robot hands

Robots don't really need hands in the same way humans do. They usually don't need the flexibility as they are designed to do a specific job. If a robot needs to pick something up it can usually use a two-fingered action, so it only needs a two-fingered hand.

For extra grip, robots can use a three-fingered hand.

Robots don't need human-like hands.

So there are millions of robots in factories. Does that also mean there are millions of robots in people's houses?

Yes, and their numbers are growing all the time as more labour-saving robots are made available for us to buy.

Why do we need robots at home?

Because doing jobs around the house can be pretty boring, so wouldn't it be good if robots could do those jobs for us? It makes life easier for humans and gives us more time for relaxing and having fun.

Here are some robots that don't mind getting their hands dirty - if they had hands that is, which they don't!

Let's start with one you might have seen: a robot **vacuum cleaner**.

They don't look anything like a conventional vacuum cleaner. They have sensors that detect obstacles, like chairs and tables.

Underneath the robot, sensors detect dirt on the floor and send a signal for it to start sucking.

The best thing is that you just leave them to it.

You can now get robot mops for tiled floors.

How about a robot that can fold your clothes for you?

Foldimate can do it twice as fast as a human, and probably a bit neater too.

Want your **windows cleaned**?

What do you mean, you've never really thought that much about it? Start thinking now because robots like this Winbot can stick to windows using suction pads and use a cloth and a squeegee like a real window cleaner.

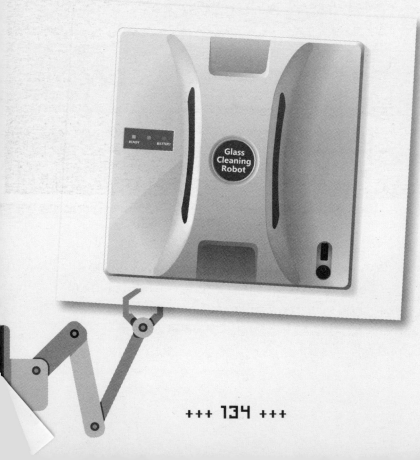

A bit like a robot vacuum cleaner, a robot **lawnmower** can be left in your garden to do its own thing.

Incidentally, 'its own thing' is cutting the grass.

When they are low on battery they head back to the charger for a top-up (just like the tortoise robots Elmer and Elsie) and even have a rain detector on them to let them know that it's time to give them a break.

Could robots replace animals as pets?

They take less looking after, as you don't have to feed them or clean up after them. But could they give you the same love and affection that we would hope to get from our pets?

Which do you prefer?

This puppy:

Or this robot dog:

It might be a tough choice, but, be honest, you probably liked the puppy best.

However, robot pets might not just be play things, they might be useful.

Like **Tega**, an educational robot developed at MIT (Massachusetts Institute of Technology) by a team led by Professor Cynthia Breazeal. Tega is a friendly-looking robot that is programmed to help children expand their vocabulary and interact with them to work on classroom projects.

The clever thing is that Tega uses a smartphone as its brain which is a bit different to other robots. Also, children can design what Tega looks like and program it to sing songs and play games too.

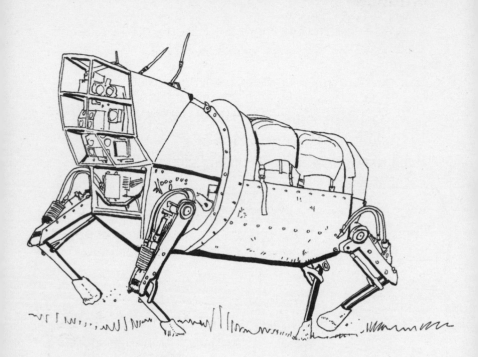

The AlphaDog

AlphaDog isn't really a pet, but it is a robot dog.

It would be good to have around especially if you're going on a long walk as AlphaDog can carry all the equipment and supplies over pretty much any kind of terrain. And if you get lost AlphaDog has GPS to find the way home.

Robocar

How else could robots improve our lives? Could a robot take us places? Yes, if it's a self-driving **car**.

Self-driving or autonomous cars already exist.

Engineers and scientists have been working on them since the 1920s.

But it wasn't until 1986 that the first one worked. It was called **Navlab**.

Navlab was a big van full of computers that couldn't go over 20mph. So it was a bit limited, but it was a good start.

Many companies are working on them now, even companies like Google, that you might not associate with making cars.

Google's driverless car has driven over **1,498,214 miles** in tests. That's a really long way, equivalent to driving to the moon and back three times.

How do driverless cars work?

Like lots of robots, they use **programming** and **sensors**.

First of all, an onboard computer has to be programmed with every driving manoeuvre that can be thought of, and then a few more just to be safe. Then **sensors** on the car need to detect what's going on around it.

Cameras detect traffic lights, read road signs and look out for other cars.

Light sensors keep the car on the road.

LIDAR stands for Light Detection and Ranging. It shines out a laser light and the sensor measures how far away an object is.

The wheels have **ultrasonic sensors** so it knows where the cars are. This helps with parking. Ultrasonic sensors measure sounds that are too high for humans to hear. They bounce sounds off objects and then use the echo to work out how far away the object is.

The Future of Robots

What will robots be like in the future?

Well, we can guess a bit, in that they will be more intelligent, able to do things more efficiently, respond to programming faster, and generally they'll just be better.

But could they replace humans altogether?

Well, let's hope not because that wouldn't be great for humans.

Seriously though, are there robots being developed that could take the place of a human?

Yes, there are and they look like these **Geminoid** robots.

Geminoid F is 165cm tall, has life-like features, and plugs into the mains.

Geminoid H1-4 is 180cm tall and uses similar technology to Geminoid F.

They each have plastic skulls, metal skeletons and silicone skin.

They both look very much like humans – in fact they are both modelled on real people, but not to replace those people. At least I hope not.

There is one thing stopping people being replaced by realistic human-like robots. And that's based on a theory called **'the uncanny valley'**. Although it has nothing to do with actual valleys.

What is it about, then?

When robots get too much like humans, for some reason we stop liking them. Look at the pictures on the previous spread. How do you feel about them?

Do you think that they look great or is there a nagging little thought that something doesn't quite seem right? That's the uncanny valley.

Because of this, robots don't tend to have faces that look exactly like humans. They might have features that look a bit like eyes or a mouth, but they don't tend to look super-realistic.

+++ **144** +++

What else can we expect from robots in the future?

How about tiny robots that can go inside your body and help kill diseases and rebuild any damage that might be in there?

Those robots are called **nanobots**.

What are nanobots?

They are robot grandmas.

OK, so they aren't robot grandmas . . . But they are possibly the next big thing and they are tiny.

Nanobots are called nanobots because they are about the size of a **nanometre**.

Whats a nanometre?

It's **one thousand millionth** of a metre.

You won't be able to see a nanobot as they'd be too small to see with an average microscope.

Everything is made up of atoms. A gang of atoms (two or more) is called a molecule. Nanobots are about the size of a molecule. If you measured a water molecule it would be about 40 million times smaller than 1cm.

Very basic nanobots already exist. In 2005 Professor James Tour and his team built a nanocar.

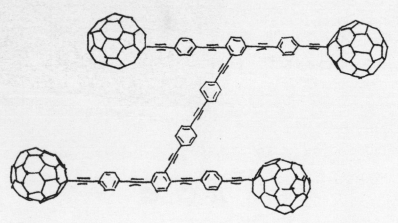

Nanocars are made of molecules with little wheels made of 60 fullerene molecules. This is seriously small. In fact it's 20,000 times thinner than a human hair.

Fullerene is a carbon molecule in the shape of a sphere. Probably why they work well as wheels.

It doesn't have a motor like a real car but it does slide down metal surfaces, just in a teeny-tiny way.

But what would nanobots do?

They are still being worked on but hopefully they will be used in medicine to help fight bacteria and viruses and also to help our bodies heal.

If more complex nanobots become a reality it could mean the end to a lot of diseases and really change how humans live their lives, all thanks to teeny-tiny robots.

Here's a picture of a nanobot:

Small, aren't they?

Brain control

The future could be full of really small robots, but what if we could get rid of remote controls and computers and control robots with our **minds**? Wouldn't that be awesome?

Will we be able to control robots with our minds?

We already can, using EEG – electroencephalography – which detects the electrical activity in our brains.

Our brains are electric?

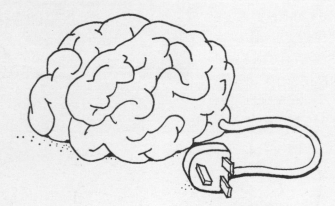

Yes, they work by sending electrical impulses.

Our brains have nerve cells in them called 'neurons'.

Neurons communicate with each other by sending out those electrical impulses.

An EEG sensor detects those impulses and interprets them so that the robot can convert them into a command to move.

If our brains are electric, are we robots?

Not really, no, though we are similar; we could be soft organic robots, at a push.

What could controlling robots with our brains be useful for?

Here's what: in 2012 the **BrainGate** project helped a woman who had suffered a stroke that had paralysed her.

Using a sensor connected to her brain to read the electrical signals, the woman was able to control a robot arm to pick up a bottle and give it to her so that she could drink from it.

In the future it could be used to control all sorts of devices from computers to wheelchairs and robots.

How to get into robotics

If you want to get into robotics there are lots of way to do it.

Become a **robotics engineer** or **technician** so you could make robots and tell them what to do. How does that sound?

You will need to study maths and science and eventually get a degree in robotics or engineering.

Or if you just want to program robots, then **computer science** is for you.

Maybe you want to connect it all together, in which case you could be a **mechatronic engineer**.

If your thing is to actually make a robot, then perhaps consider becoming a **mechanical engineer**.

But the best way to start is by tinkering with **your own robots** at home using Lego Mindstorms, Arduino kits or Sphero's, or a Raspberry Pi.

There are loads more robot kits available, or if you fancy the challenge, why not build something from scratch?

If you're not sure how, there are plenty of step-by-step guides on the web you can check out.

Good Luck!

Answers

Page 32

None of the automatons is fake – they are all real robots.

Page 41

They can all be programmed, except for the spoon (at least as far as we know at the moment!).

Picture Credits

(t = top, c = centre, b = bottom, l = left)

Pages 9, 11, 14 (b), 16, 63, 71, 90, 92, 93, 102, 105, 106, 109, 110, 111 (t, c, b), 112, 113, 115 (t, b), 116, 117 (t), 121 (b), 122 (t), 126, 130, 131 (t, b), 132, 134, 135, 136 (c, b), 141, 144, 147 all Shutterstock; pages 10 (b), 12 (b), 17, 28, 29 (t), 42, 43, 44, 45, 47, 48, 49, 50, 51, 53, 57 (b), 66, 75 (t), 79 (b-l), 84, 85, 86 (b), 117 (b), 120 and 127 all copyright © Science Museum/Science & Society Picture Library; page 8, 12 (t), 21, 27, 30, 101, 140 copyright © Wikimedia Commons; page 86 (t) copyright © Bletchley Park Trust/ Science & Society Picture Library; page 95, 98 and 125 copyright © NASA; pages 97, 142 and 143 copyright © Getty Images; page 100 copyright © European Space Agency; page 124 copyright © National Aeronautics & Space Administration/Science & Society Picture Library. All rights reserved.

Glossary

Actuator: the part of the robot that makes it move like a muscle on a human

Algorithm: a set of rules or instructions often used in computer programming

Atom: the smallest part of an element – consisting of a nucleus orbited by electrons – which still has the chemical properties of the element

Automaton: a mechanical version of a modern robot

Babbage, Charles: (1791–1871) the inventor of the first mechanical computer

Battery: an energy source made up of electrochemical cells

Binary: a number system that uses 0 or 1

Cam: a rotating, shaped piece of metal

Celsius: a temperature scale named for Anders Celsius in which freezing water is 0 degrees and boiling water is 100 degrees

CO_2: the symbol for carbon dioxide, which contains one carbon atom and two oxygen atoms

Cog: a wheel with teeth in it

Density: how tightly packed something is

Diagram: a technical drawing, often used to help explain something

Einstein, Albert: (1879–1955) the physicist who first theorized that matter and energy are the same thing and that time and space are the same thing

Electricity: a form of energy that can flow from one thing to another

Electron: a subatomic particle with a negative electric charge

Electronic: the use of electrical circuits in technology

Experiment: a test or series of tests carried out in order to find answers

Force: something that exerts a push or pull on an object

Fusion: the process of combining atomic nuclei, resulting in an enormous amount of energy being released

Galileo Galilei: (1564-1642) an Italian astronomer and physicist

Gas: a fluid substance like air, which expands freely and fills the space around it however big it is

Gear: a wheel with teeth in it that usually connects to a another wheel with teeth in it of a different size

Gravity: the force that pulls all things with a mass towards each other

Hardware: the solid bits that make up a computer

Heat: a type of energy indicated through temperature

Helium: a type of gas that is lighter than air

Humanoid: something that resembles a human

Hydrogen: a chemical element that is normally a gas or a part of water

Ice: the solid state of water

Lovelace, Ada: (1815-1852) a mathematician

Mass: how much of something there is

Mechanical: a process, or part of a machine

Molecule: the combination of the elements that make up a compound

NASA: National Aeronautics and Space Administration

Neutron: a particle in the nucleus of an atom

Nuclear: referring to atomic nuclei, as is nuclear energy

Oxygen: an element that is part of the air we breathe

Particle: a really tiny piece of something

Pressure: the excursion of force on something

Programming: writing instructions to get a computer or robot to do something

Proton: a positively charged particle found in the nucleus of an atom

Pulley: a wheel used with a rope to change the direction of a force

Reaction: a response or force that is equal or opposite to another force

Relativity: according to Galileo, relativity shows that the laws of physics remain the same no matter where you are

Robot: a machine that can be programmed to do complicated things. (Seriously, you should've paid more attention to the rest of the book!)

Sensor: something that detects things like smoke, light, sound, etc.

Software: the programs that tell computers and robots what to do

Solar sail: a theoretical device similar to a wind sail that catches solar radiation to propel a ship. One day solar sail may power a spacecraft

Space-time: a way of describing the universe in which there are four dimensions: three of space and one of time. It is associated with Einstein's theories

Sun: the big, hot thing in the sky

Temperature: how cold or hot something is

Valve: something used in old electical devices to control electric current

Weight: how heavy something is